TURNER BROOKS: WORK

Turner Brooks: Work

with essays by

Ross Anderson

Kent Bloomer

Turner Brooks

Jonathan Schell

PRINCETON ARCHITECTURAL PRESS

Published by

Princeton Architectural Press

37 East 7th Street

New York, New York 10003

(212) 995-9620

© 1995 Princeton Architectural Press, Inc.

ISBN 1-56898-031-0

First edition

Printed and bound in Canada by Friesen Printers

Book design and editing by Allison Saltzman

on the front cover: the Lombard/Miller House, photographed by Cervin Robinson

Library of Congress Cataloging-in-Publication Data

Brooks, Turner, 1943–

Turner Brooks: Work / with essays by Turner Brooks . . . [et al.].

- -1st ed.

p.   cm.

ISBN 1-56898-031-0 : $27.95

1. Brooks, Turner, 1943– - - Themes, motives.

2. Brooks, Turner, 1943– - - Criticism and interpretation.

3. Regionalism in architecture - - New England.

4. Architecture, Domestic - - Shingle style - - United States - - Influence.

5. Vernacular architecture - - New England - - Influence.

I. Title.

NA737.B69A4   1994

720 '.92 - - dc20   94-38753

CIP

For a free catalog of other books published by Princeton Architectural Press, call toll free (800) 458-1131

Contents

TURNER BROOKS: WORK

Introduction   Turner Brooks

I remember, as a child, taking great lumps of clay and making what my friends and I called ghost houses. We ran our fingers deep into the mass and made chambers far inside. These could be lit subtly by sky-lit passages. Tunnels connected to tunnels, which connected to deeply buried rooms that couldn't be seen at all. Some tunnels had grand portals for entries, others were humble, others hidden and secret. One could not actually travel into these seemingly sacred spaces, but empathetically one *could*. Sometimes, as in Kafka's *The Burrow*, the passages became so complex that one actually lost track of exactly where they went or how they connected. That is when they became "ghost houses," and took on a mysterious power and life of their own. These ghost houses are related in my mind to houses I knew as a child, and to my work later on.

I like buildings that remain mysterious and ambiguous and that one must journey through—sometimes repeatedly—before beginning to comprehend them. I have a strong memory of my grandparents' old Victorian house in Pittsburgh, which held within it endless possible connecting journeys. The one I particularly liked started in the pitch-dark basement filled with bins of coal and a demonic roaring furnace with portals glowing orange. From there I would travel upwards to the main floor through grand rooms with light-filled bays, past fireplaces with shimmering tiles reflecting the dusky light of rooms wrapped in dark floral wallpaper. Mantels and shelves held arrays of family photos, books, and trinkets that gleamed. Turning from the grand generous stair that ascended up to a landing with a seat under a leaded window, I would pass through a dark, varnished, swinging door into the narrow passage of an old pantry, where, turning again through another door, I came into a dark, wood-paneled, narrow, winding, creaking stair which led, finally, to the attic. Here, under the steep boarded roof was the smell of hot wood and pitch and mustiness, and all around were piles of things—great chests, steamer trunks, furniture, mirrors, framed pictures of ancestors in military attire—the accumulated stuff of generations. Here in the soft amber light were the ancestral relics and collective memories of the family whose present members bustled about in the rooms below.

Fig. 2

The great fable *The Little House*, by the children's book author Virginia Lee Burton, seems to have forever influenced my view of inhabiting the space of the landscape. It is the story of a farmhouse in a landscape that changes violently around it. The house starts its life sited on a rounded knoll in an idyllic pastoral countryside where, as the seasons change, its occupants engage in the typical seasonal pursuits of farmers. But as the pages turn to reveal a quiet, peaceful life, one notices alarming dots (buildings) gathering on the surrounding hills. Another page is turned, and suddenly there is the shocking image of a road, laid brutally across the little rounded knoll,

Fig. 3

directly in front of the house. The rhythm of farm life is immediately interrupted. The barn is replaced by a gas station. The surrounding landscape is then relentlessly invaded by buildings arriving in ever-denser waves. The little house is surrounded by suburbia, then it is impacted by brownstones, and finally it is abandoned, squeezed into a canyon between the towering flanks of 1930s skyscrapers. A subway is built underneath it and an elevated train trestle above it. The house is finally rescued from this claustrophobic predicament by the distant offspring of the farmer who originally built it. When the house is placed on a truck, the frantic activity of the city (including the elevated train) halts ceremoniously in acknowledgment of its departure as it begins its journey back into the country. Figure 2 shows the house taking this journey—a kind of evolution of its life in reverse in which it quests another knoll where it can exist again in peace. But the end of the story is ambiguous, and I remember scanning the horizon for the inevitable encroachment of dots on the distant hills, which would signal that the same process would happen all over again. Of course, houses are actually moving all the time all around us. Figure 3 shows a prickly little Victorian house being pulled out of its site in the town of Brandon, Vermont to browse in the surrounding country. As a container of an interior space, this house, like the "little house" of the story, remained intact and the same, while the landscape outside changed wildly.

Journeying with my family between the city and the country was a part of the ritual of my early life. Grand Central Station, that great swelling space hovering over the mysterious labyrinth of passageways, seemed to connect to everything *out there*, and for me was the womb from which the country in northwest Vermont was born. Gliding out from its steamy depths into the night, snugly encapsulated in the cozy upper berth of the sleeper car, I would wake with the great wide landscape of the Champlain Valley flashing by outside the windows. Or Friday nights, snuggled in the fuzzy-textured back seat of the '39 Ford—it seemed to just contain my body under the rounded roof sweeping over me—we drove out of the city across the George Washington Bridge and into the woods of New Jersey. Soon we would approach, illuminated by the headlights, a solitary, ghostly husk of a tiny dwelling. Inside, we groped in the dark until we found the kerosene

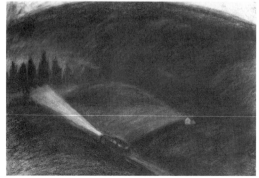

Figs. 4a–d

heater. Flickeringly, the interior would start to glow and grow fragrant, the space opening up and becoming warm and palpable. Sunday evening, ensconced again in the back seat of the Ford, my father, the lights from the instrument panel reflecting off the side of his face, would invent a mystery story as he guided the car through the night landscape, back towards the distant glow of the city (Figs. 4a–d).

When I moved to rural Vermont I found myself drawn to some of the more shacky and scruffy specimens of buildings—particularly the buildings that seemed to hold within them the image of movement, as if they were motoring across the landscape under their own power. But these structures, unlike the "little house," actually look like they are *supposed* to move. In the context of a landscape in turbulent transition, where the old agricultural order is disintegrating rapidly, the physical lightness, the visual sense of being in motion, the quality of being unfixed to a particular site, all seems very appropriate. These buildings don't root themselves into the landscape; they look "right" moving through it. Alone on the landscape as a ship is alone on the sea, they make their own way across it. The relationship of their inhabitants to the land is itself much more tenuous than that of their farmer predecessors; mostly they drive off somewhere else to work.

The elegant shack in figure 5, a combination sugar house/green house made of ad hoc materials, appears, with its double-barreled stack, to be chugging across the landscape. The house in figure 6 seems to be an amphibious creature, questing a puddle in which to float. I like the Ticonderoga, figure 7, the last paddle-wheel steamboat on Lake Champlain, crossing the landscape five miles from the nearest water. The trailers (40s and 50s vintage) are all about movement—their stretched, taut forms hovering across the landscape. Figure 8 might move off towards the left if its gang plank were pulled back. Figure 9 holds the memory of the road and movement in its gently rounded rear and forward-leaning front—the memory commemorated poignantly in the embellished "forehead" ornament of the picket fence, which has the aspect of a wise, furrowed brow. Figure 10 nestles cozily like an egg in the shrubbery. The blue and white trailer in figure 11 becomes a piece of a harmonious pastoral landscape. The trailer is there now, like the cows, but could move off or disappear without a trace.

Figs. 5–8

Fig. 9

These buildings all have a very different relationship to the landscape from that of the tradition-al farmhouse. The farmhouse possesses the landscape by extending its elements—fences, walls, barns, sheds, cultivated fields, cleared meadows, organized wood lots—out to meet the natural landscape. It is a man-made composition, with the geometry of the cultivated landscape emanat-ing outward from the abstract box of the house into the natural world. The agricultural land-scape acts as a middle ground between the dwelling and the larger natural landscape. Now, as farms deteriorate, fields turn to brush, the forest encroaches, the middle ground deteriorates, and the grand clarity of this classic composition is lost. There is almost no such thing as a new farm-house. New houses are generally the same abstract boxes, but marooned without the middle ground to steady them and knit them into the larger landscape. The last vestige of the man-made landscape—the lawn—does not seem to be quite enough.

Figs. 10, 11

Figs. 12–14

I have borrowed a lot from the old vernacular architecture that still inhabits this landscape so gracefully. Often left with only remnants of their old agricultural order around them, I found myself particularly admiring of the houses that were tiny but at the same time made grand and exaggerated gestures. Figure 12 is one of these. Its roof, on the left, sweeps low to the ground over its little private door—barely five-and-a-half-feet tall—while simultaneously, it swells up on the right into a gable over a magnificently scaled and elegant central portal, huge on the little facade, and makes a generous public gesture towards the road. Figure 13 shows another small house that pulls itself up proudly to confront the road with its handsomely ornamented front porch. This contrasts with the purely functional porch on the rear side, over which the roof dips down very low. The house in figure 14 has a wonderfully gentle, welcoming, figural form. From the central body the shed roofs stretch out gently like arms to hold open the space of the porch that embraces you in its cool shade amid the softly floating laundry that embellishes it. These buildings are related in that they are all small in fact, but make gestures that are large. They are at once humble and grand.

I also love the materials in which these structures are clothed, that seem to reinforce the largeness of their personalities. For example, the wide, generous trim boards anchoring the windows and doors firmly into the wall of tiny clapboards. Or the doors with massive lintels, sometimes extending well up into the space of the second floor, and the gigantic frieze boards and corner boards and skirt boards, binding these little houses compactly together and increasing their toughness and scale, so that they are at home in the large-scale landscape. These little houses knew how to dress themselves.

The houses I have designed have no extended man-made agricultural landscape surrounding them to anchor them in the bigger natural landscape. Instead it is the landscape at large, and as it is found, upon which the house acts independently and by itself. I see my buildings as compact bodies—taut, stretched, swelling objects—with a strong directional sense, isolated on a landscape which they inhabit easily, but from which they read as distinctly separate. Often built on the scruffy abandoned edges of this great agricultural landscape, they hover slightly, and are "placed" on the landscape without any presumption or ambition of transforming it. They are simply there, containers that outside their own tight wrappers assume no accommodation to or from their surroundings. Like the trailers, shacks, and boats from which they partially descend, they are launched directly onto the landscape and must make their way through it alone (Fig. 15).

Fig. 15

That I like the "object" quality of my buildings seen separately from a particular site is demonstrated by the many model junkyards inhabiting the shelves in my office (Fig. 16). In fact I have some reverence for these junkyards, and don't ever clean them up. I have photographed models of these "uprooted" buildings making their way through both country and city landscapes.

Figs. 16–19

Figure 17 shows a model with a wind-up motor, wheels, and ski on the front, struggling uphill in the country—a kind of "low rider." Figure 18 shows the same house in a city made out of blocks by my kids. Figure 19 shows a house model floating in the bathroom sink with a candle-powered Pop Pop boat coming up on the starboard flank.

In 1976, I actually designed a house with *no* particular site in mind. This was for a friend who, although owning no land himself, had many friends who did, and between whose estates he planned to move his modest domicile. He had welded together two mighty sled runners and needed a house to bolt onto them that was eight feet wide, sixteen feet long and no taller than fourteen feet (so that it could fit under power lines and most bridges). Over land, it slid on the runners pulled by two tractors swishing easily through the tall grass (Fig. 20). Wheels could be bolted to the runners for travel on roads. Unlike actual trailers that lower their "skirts" to the ground and rarely ever move again, this dwelling has moved often, has changed owners at least four times, and was last seen on its wheels heading across the border into Canada.

Fig. 20

I like to draw my buildings in atmospheric conditions in which they appear to be steaming and hissing along as if passing through the landscape under their own power. These are nocturnal visions, sometimes made during the design process as an image of how I imagine a building will look, but more often made after construction is finished as a kind of "ideal" version of the project, never quite attainable in real life. The specific site melts away and the building acts alone, at once looming and cozy in the darkness.

Top: Figs. 21, 22; bottom: Figs. 23a, b

At the same time I think my buildings *engage* the landscape even as they appear to move through it. They make gestures across it. Their directional sense propels them towards and connects them to various landscape events: a cleft in the hills, a sight-line to a distant mountain, or simply an alignment with a valley (Fig. 15). Or it could be a man-made thing, as is the case with the Chapman House in Idaho, which slips between two Ponderosa pine trees to aim at a railroad trestle crossing a depression in the landscape some two miles away—the only visible object out there in the wheat fields and prairie grass (Fig. 21). The entire plan of this building is pulled to this distant trestle as if by a thread strung along the center of the plan; it draws the entrance inward and telescopes the living room out towards it. The immediate smaller-scale topography of the site also comes into play. The Glazebrook House (Fig. 22), for example, is stretched out along the top of a small esker that curls out of the woods into the field that the house inhabits. The Chapman House is placed so that it rides the crest of the last of a series of knolls that break like waves on the prairie to the north. The Rockwell House (Figs. 23a, b) also seems to ride a swell in the gently undulating topography of its site. The Sheldon House (Fig. 24a, b) shifts its direction at midlength to head off, between two knolls, towards the nearest visible inlet of Lake Champlain.

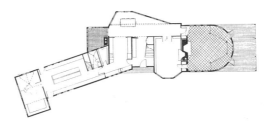

Figs. 24a, b

The landscape is also engaged from within the building, where, from certain locations, there is the sense that one is guiding or steering a vessel. Standing in the kitchen of the Glazebrook House and looking through the studio and out down the tracks to the kiln shed, one has the sense of *driving* this house along the ridge of the esker and out into the swelling fields beyond (Fig. 25). In the Chapman House, one is aware of the connection to the trestle out in the prairie as one enters the building. Most of my houses have a kind of control room or ship's bridge, from which one sees out over the body of the house into the landscape (Figs. 26a, b, c, d).

Fig. 25

Figs. 26a–d

From the outside, my buildings are perceived as distinct things on the landscape. But inside, they enfold one in a series of spaces in which there is the possibilty, while wandering through them, of becoming, briefly, lost. I like to think that one finds oneself again through a series of small discoveries that increasingly make sense of where one is in relation to the building as a whole, as well as to the landscape outside. This *whole* is discovered in the course of the journey around and through the building, as one circulates in and out of its various internal currents and eddies, while also finding views to the outside. There is a sense of possessing the building as an assembled, complete body. It becomes not only comprehensible but exhilarating, as a vessel that surrounds you, contains you, and connects you with the landscape outside.

I have often described my buildings in bodily terms as creatures with heads, limbs, tails. As one walks around them, elements stretch out, retract back in, folding and unfolding as if one is encircling a recumbent beast. A bay projects out, a wall rotates towards a view, but all is held tightly, elastically, back to the central body of the building. The building responds to the site and landscape as a body that makes a gesture. Many of the great vehicles that I like are themselves like creatures of some sort (Fig. 27). The curved roof on the McLane House, which in a nautical or vehicular analogy might be a cowling over the engine, becomes a swelling chest of a body, the bay window a curled up haunch that gives a sense of the building crouching, and the gable which could be the cab of a locomotive, is also the head of a beast (Fig. 28). Inhabiting the head (brain) is analogous to inhabiting a locomotive's cab or a ship's bridge. In the Sheldon House, which slips through the landscape long and train-like, the master bedroom protrudes out like a head

Figs. 27, 28

from the hunched shoulders of the roof that stretches out like a limb over the porch (Figs. 29a, b, c, d). The bend in the house's plan is like the hinge between railroad cars, but more like a joint between torso and legs. In the Lombard/Miller House, the third floor study is another bridge or head-like element. The tilted hat of the roof gives it an unmistakably directional yearning as it rises out of the main box or body of the house (Fig. 26d). The Gates Center at the College of the Atlantic has a more crustacean look (Figs. 30a, b). The main body is the large swelling ribbed

Figs. 29a, b, c, d

space of the meeting hall. The faculty offices and gallery bend around in a sort of segmented tail. Here, the head is the tiny lobby space containing a gigantic fireplace (Figs. 31a, b) to and in which relics and artifacts of the school are to be attached and imbedded. It becomes a repository of memory and acts as a brain for this creature-like building. If a creature, the building remains, as in the vehicle or boat metaphor, an object separate from the landscape, waiting to move.

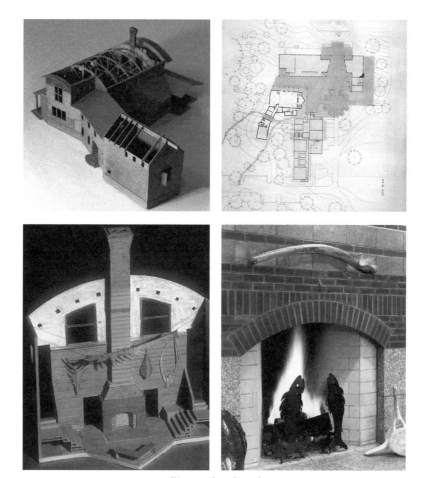

Figs. 30a, b, and 31a, b

Figs. 32, 33, 34a, b

The small-scale "objects" included in this book weave between vehicular and creature imagery. Il Risorgimento (Fig. 32) is the most anthropomorphic of the lot, although it has the wings of a creature and wheels of a vehicle. The Hovering Creatures may be metamorphoses of buildings, dragon flies, and lobster boats (Fig. 33), while the model series for the retired lobsterman shows some sort of insect/ferry boat hybrid (Figs. 34a, b).

Beast-like or vehicular, my buildings are compact forms in the landscape with interior spaces that are expansive and full but at the same time contained. I like peering into them at night from the outside. It is at night that they seem most like elastic containers of space that are distinctly interior and separate from the landscape outside. From some views they look particularly like boats gliding across a meadow with light pouring out the windows and reflecting off the grasses outside. They remind me at other times of the warm interior of a nut. They are light-weight, wood-frame constructions, tightly wrapped in an elastic skin that expands outward and contracts inward to form the interior space. One has the sense that the landscape is kept at bay, revealed through windows that are large enough to absorb the view but never break the continuity of the walls which contain the interior space and allow the building to maintain its object quality, floating free on the landscape.

Fig. 35

The McLane House (Fig. 35) doesn't move, but people remark that it looks especially like an abandoned diesel locomotive, and that, of course, pleases me. Other people see boat analogies and still others think it most resembles a shoe (pleasing me less!). Like many of my houses, it is stretched and taut, hovers slightly, and appears to be gliding ever so slowly over the ground. The skirt board at its base seems to keep it as an object from touching the ground. The horizontal trim board at the second-floor level both pulls the eaves of the shed roof and curved end together along the length of the building and, at the same time, emphasizes the building's elastic quality. These trim motifs come both from trailers and from traditional vernacular houses. Although I of course spent hours siting the house in a very specific spot, which had to do both with how it engaged the landscape as an object and how the landscape was viewed from within, the "thought" is that it could actually be anyplace...almost. It looks to me just right on the landscape sliding through this small valley, inflecting and gesturing to the hills. It is built on what has become the typical site for me: at the unkempt edge of an agricultural landscape growing up with weeds and brush. The power lines are nearby and, had I been allowed by the utility company, would have passed directly over the roof as they do with a street car. The owners tend to the landscape only as an aesthetic issue and agree with me that the generally weedy surroundings look good with the house.

Once in the door of the McLane House, turning left one passes down a short, low-ceilinged hall to enter the central space of the house, which contains living, dining and kitchen areas (see page 59). This space, which opens outward and upwards, is like a bay window that has expanded to become the complete living space of the house. It is a small but generous room with walls joined at obtuse angles, pushing outward, as if forced by a pressure from the interior to contain the space. The truss seems not so much to bear the weight of the roof (as it actually does) as to hold the walls apart. The walls are pulled paper-thin around the over-scaled, double-hung windows. The chair rail wraps around the space like a stretched rubber band. The roof starts low and builds over the truss, rising up to reveal the space of the second floor through a huge interior window. While it is a single space contained in this elastic fashion, it is also complex. There are small inhabitable pockets and bays that slide out and join the larger intervening space of which they are a part. It is a room that engages the body as one wanders through its various realms and corners.

From this space, the main hall passes by a narrow, almost hidden, bending passage to a first-floor bedroom, and then leads to a stair that ascends under the curve of the roof. Sliding up in the curve one passes a tiny nook or cabinet for sleeping reminiscent of the sleeping berth in a train. Once on the second floor, one can turn into the master bedroom that looks back through a window to the space of the living area below. Or one can continue up the stair, which squeezes to a very narrow dimension, twisting its way up to the third floor. Here, looking out over the descending roof with the dual smoke stacks, one feels firmly in control of the destiny of the house as it heads out across the landscape towards the shifting patterns of meadows that lie ahead. Here one has a sense of possessing the house as a whole. It is as if one inhabits its brain, and senses the building as an intimate extension of one's own body. If there were a steering wheel, it would be from here that one would navigate the house through the landscape. It is spaces such as these that bring me back to the original vehicles that transported me as a child out into the country, sliding through the night, the landscape wonderfully revealed through the small rounded windows of a cozy upper berth in the train or back seat of a car. Virginia Lee Burton's "little house," too, was a traveling container, cozily itself wherever it was. From car, train, and house, the landscape is revealed from the interior of an object that contains the body wrapped in a space snugly and firmly, within which one feels secure in the larger landscape viewed outside.

Fig. 36a, b

The Brooks House (Figs. 36a–f), my own domicile, has an exhausting, battering history of additions, alterations, and drastic amputations. But in its present incarnation it is in many ways the sister ship in spirit to the McLane House. It is also a "shaped" elastic space, expanding and

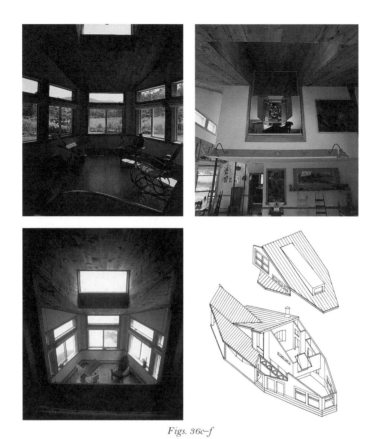

Figs. 36c–f

contracting, bowing out, and pulling in, to accommodate the spatial configuration of the interior (Fig. 36b). It is anchored down the center of its length by an axis, which starts, I claim (grandly), at the depression between a double-peaked mountain some six miles away. This is perhaps distantly inspired by the Horns of Hymettus of Vincent Scully's *The Earth the Temple and the Gods.* This axis cuts through the living room, and then rises up, aligned under the long "dust-pan" dormer that erupts gradually from the roof, passes through the master bedroom above, crosses over the single peak of the headboard, and then ends in the cabinet or ancestral reliquary, which is in the exact center of the house (Fig. 36c). This reliquary is filled with strange artifacts—masks, spirits, and other assorted jumbled objects of ancestral caliber (Fig. 36d), and is connected by a tiny, narrow passageway to the children's bedrooms behind it. This mysterious cabinet has played an active part in the life of the house. A drama in the living room put on by my kids and their friends involved the opening of an ancient "Egyptian" sarcophagus out of which suddenly flew a startling flapping silvery mylar spirit of a mummified creature. Fluttering around the living room, it went up through the bedroom and disappeared into the reliquary. It is from the space along this axis, both in the living room and the master bedroom, that one feels especially connected and bodily merged with this house as it glides across a meadow, aligned along its axis, to the mountain in the distance. It is a house too impoverished to have a true attic or cellar, but its light-filled bays, its narrow twisting stairs, and its secret passageways bring back memories of the ancestral house in Pittsburgh. In the bow-like space facing east, one sits on axis with the mountain, clearly in control of the building as it heads into the landscape, while the mysteries and histories of the house are enfolded in the labyrinth behind your back.

I don't think of the spaces I make as empty. Rather they are pulled, stretched, or otherwise shaped. At best, they are full and energized. I like to think that the ones that are well shaped would survive even if the walls, floors, and roofs that define them were removed. They might exist as currents, whirlpools, waves, compressions, or expansions that are flowing up, down, and around, causing drafts and eddies. They would still be inhabited by reverberations and sounds, such as those made by the flapping of the mylar spirit questing its ancestral reliquary.

Figures in the Landscape   Kent Bloomer

The ideals that drive works of architecture are often expressed in photographs. Sometimes they are best expressed in photographs. That is not so of the architecture of Turner Brooks, at least not so for this writer. Only by approaching, walking around, entering, and circulating and sitting in his buildings could I comprehend the scope of their extraordinary magic. His work is utterly three-dimensional.

Listening to Brooks extol upon the virtues of the landscape in which his buildings are placed requires being in that landscape and focusing attentively on some distant precipice, flood plain, or mountain range towards which he gestures with an outstretched hand. When he is satisfied that you have seen and paid respect to those edges, it is likely that his attention will move further outward to the *other side* of them, to the invisible and mythical realms that he refers to as the "Midwest" or the "Atlantic." You are required to concentrate and hone in on those edges and outer worlds before you become licensed to discuss the very square foot that you are standing or sitting upon. Those distant forces, elastically perceived, are vectors poised to carve and shape the tranquil buildings designed by Turner Brooks.

It should be noted that Brooks does not describe his architecture as being tranquil; he imagines his buildings to be virtually moving over the landscape. Such an image suggests restlessness or an absence of repose. Yet, despite architectural expressions of a body and head alerted to the surround, his works are serene and impressed onto a place. I suspect that Brooks is talking about his own sense of being an explorer wandering through the landscape. He projects this sensibility onto his work during the process of designing. The process is one of restless exploration but each building is a resolution and a settlement.

The houses designed by Turner Brooks are proud and elegant figures in the landscape. The first and most important impression each of them provides is that of a venerable, classically regional, and mysteriously "typical" domicile. They do not present themselves as reactionary or rhetorical. Nor do they present themselves as modern "sculptures" despite the fact that their bodies are formed down-to-the-inch by the demands characteristic of a virtuoso sculptor. They remain truly conventional works of architecture that simultaneously perform as rigorously sculptured volumes pervading and being pervaded by the greater landscape.

These multiple agendas of architectural classicality, sculptural resolution, and engagement with the landscape propose an extremely complex process of ordering.

The Peek House

Because these words are in a book and we are not walking around one of Turner Brooks's buildings I shall concentrate on the composition of one building that I believe is fundamentally characteristic of many of the others. The Peek House is one of the smallest, most distilled, and most suitable for abstract analysis.

At first glance the profile of the house seems to possess a regional classicism, as though it had been there for a long time, settled in a field and resisting the wind and rain (Fig. 2). From the approach it is anchored by a small two-story gabled "tower" with an ordinary porch to the right and a long set-backed and "accrued" or distended shed to the left. In front of the shed there is a one-story lateral extension of the main elevation in the form of a shallow "saddlebag" with small kitchen windows and an entry door. All of these elements, taken separately, are quite typical to Vermont at least in regard to the sizing of the types of windows, doors, clapboards, trim, and posts. The elements seem at first glance to be organized in a customary way.

However the juxtaposition of these elements is actually unusual. One of the ways of characterizing the composition of the Peek House is to say that it is a continuous in-the-round rendition

Following page: Figs. 1–8
Top to bottom, left to right: model and views of the Peek House
from the north, west, southwest, south, southeast, east, and northeast

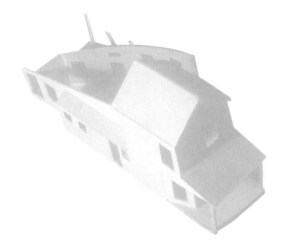

of dynamic symmetries that are carefully and ingeniously choreographed. If something on an elevation shifts to the right of the center of gravity, something else shifts to the left. If a void is dug into the central mass, a solid element nearby will protrude outward. If a mass pushes upward to establish a vertical mark, some horizontal mass will distend outward as a reaction. And while this may be partially understood by studying the rectangular or polar elevations of front, back, and side, some of the most extraordinary inflections of dynamic symmetry occur along the diagonal axis or from the three-quarter viewpoints. If you walk around the Peek House (or any of Brooks's houses) with the architect and fail to notice those climactic moments in which the front elevation and side elevations fold together, you might be grabbed by the shoulders and given a lesson in the ways to experience a three-dimensional form in the round. It will be an important lesson.

Let us approach the front (north) elevation and orient ourselves to the entrance (Fig. 2). The entrance door is located nearly at the midway point between left and right ends. The opening is on the lowly saddlebag rather than within the imposing base of the tower. Immediately this sets the elements of the facade into a dynamic symmetry in which the right side of the entry ascends upward while the left side hunkers down. Insuring that the tower doesn't retain its ancestral authority Brooks's further disarms it by cutting away its lower right-hand corner and swinging a segment of the wall inward. This act of carving away the frontal plane neatly establishes a sliver of covered space that, in conjunction with the space underneath the porch, defines a negative one-story rectangle on the right-hand side of the facade that counterbalances the positive one-story rectangle of the saddlebag to the left. Thus the front of the house is at once ordinary in its tranquility, yet extraordinary as its surface zigs and zags.

Moving around to the west porch elevation (Fig. 3), there is again a seemingly typical gable-end that has been slightly disarmed, or should we say dislegged, by having its lower left corner carved away. That incision takes the end elevation out of square and equilibrium, and thus the two large windows move to the right as players in a balancing act bent on stabilizing the wall. The weight of the small rear entrance wall further anchors the ever-so-slightly unstable visual composition of this elevation.

As we move around to the southwest corner (Fig. 4), we can see that both the northwest and the southeast corners of the building were carved away from their rectangular footprints. Yet the entire building seems tranquil and protected as the porch roofs to the left and right of the diagonal flap downward like the protective wings of a mother bird.

Looking at the back of the building from the south (Fig. 5), the masses momentarily become unlocked, although they remain firmly secured to the ground and anchored below grade by the basement wall and doorway that serves as a submerged masonry plinth located at the virtual center of gravity. Normally Brooks prefers to employ the trim board at the base of the main floor as the critical and final lower boundary of his compositions. Perhaps for that reason, the basement doorway and window appear as though they were exhumed from another world beneath the house rather than born into the life of the rear elevation.

Moving around to the southeast corner and looking back up to the Peek House (Fig. 6), one can witness the kind of diabolical inflection of elevations that the architect treasures. The house, although seeming to be convoluted and skewed from this viewpoint, remains firm and absolutely fixed in the landscape.

It is noteworthy that Brooks develops all of his architecture at the outset in models. His thoughts congeal in three dimensions before he begins to study and refine the two-dimensional plans and sections. It seems that his plans are extruded from the volumes rather than the customary other way around.

Nevertheless the plans become carefully resolved, and in the Peek House the plan reveals the internal motive behind the sweeping curve of the southeast window wall. After entering the house through the front door, one is gently turned by the splayed stair wall and kitchen wall to face the great boundary that radially sweeps the southeastern quadrant. The boundary arrests the physical path of entry as it allows a panoramic "movement of the mind" into the lake and the hills beyond the lake. It provides a sequence of openings that are not merely constituted to provide the popular and hypnotic water view of real-estate fame, but rather to catapult the mind right over the lake into the "beyond," which I suppose Brooks might point out would include, in this case, the "North Atlantic." Looking at the plan, one can see that the building presents the aspirations of a frozen actor performing a geometric ballet with the distant valleys and peaks of the rolling Vermont landscape.

A functional analysis of the plan also reveals a sensible and economic arrangement of space. A small house, with an upstairs and a downstairs bedroom sequestered in the tower, it reserves most of the interior as an open place that incorporates a front entry vestibule, a rear entry vestibule, and an east-side porch entry vestibule that doubles as a dining room. Thus, with three vestibules, the ceremonial or liminal rituals of entry and exit are endowed with space while opening directly into the splendor of the main salon. At the edges of that salon, the privacy of the bathroom and kitchen is elegantly zoned and articulated. In short, every square inch of the plan is studied, economized, and designed with an old-world grandeur hovering in the shell of a windblown Vermont collage of vernacular sheds.

Some Other Houses

To analyze all of Turner Brooks's houses is to find the same elements of economy, classicality, sculptural resolution, and pervasion of the landscape that epitomize the Peek House. Most of the other houses are constituted by a dynamic symmetry and contrapposto between the plan and the outstanding and precipitous elements of the rural or "urban" landscape as evidenced, for example, by the Sheldon House, the Salvatore House, the McLane House, and the Gates Center at the College of the Atlantic.

Top to bottom, left to right:
Figs. 9a, b, c and Figs. 10 a, b, c

Yet the forms of some other houses obey the authority ordained by strong axes of symmetry that inflect inward to a fixed centerpoint. In the facade of the Chelminski House (Figs. 9a–c) this condition results in a tension between the symmetry of the front door-attic-chimney-peak ensemble and the front steps that seem to have been pushed to the left by the energy of a drastic 40-degree slice through the right side of the body. The Fuisz House (Figs. 10a–c) exhibits a similar tension between the nearly absolute formality of its main facade and the asymmetrical appendages of bays and extended porch. The principal axis of this house reaches out to a juncture in the distance that virtually connects New York City with the Midwest—while the appendages engage the program and the intimate landscape.

Occasionally, however, the plans are frozen into the stark bilateral symmetry of the Chapman House, the Humstone House, and the Hurd House (Figs. 11–13). These seemingly radical formations in the lexicon of Brooks's otherwise dynamic choreography may be partially explained by the authority of distant man-made elements that impose immense visual axes of symmetry.

Top to bottom, left to right:
Figs. 11, 12, 13a, b

In the Chapman House (Fig. 11) there is a bridge spanning a vale on a straight line about two miles out on the prairie, on an axis from the center of the rear bay window. It would seem that the bridge has already disciplined the gently rolling landscape, and the unrelenting bisymmetry of the house is paying homage to that masterful stroke.

Similarly, within the treescape between the Humstone House (Fig. 13b), which is a renovated barn, and Lake Champlain there is a clearing that forms a long and straight "highway of the mind" between the building and the lake (Fig. 13a). The alignment of the front door beneath a small tower and trompe-l'oeil gable at dead-center of the mass reinforces that rational and man-made axis.

Unlike the Chapman and Humstone Houses, however, the orientation of the bilateral and commanding rear elevation of the Hurd House (Fig. 12), which is located in a descending field between mountainous hilltops, is set askew to the distant Lake Champlain, Adirondack ridge, and "Midwest" beyond. In the absence of a man-made axis or even a spectacular cleavage or peak in the mountainous horizon, there is no overt preexisting geometry governing the symmetry. Indeed the Hurd House, in its moment of isolation, seems humbled, turned aside, and miniaturized by the grandeur and sublimely picturesque asymmetry of the cascading surround. I suspect therefore, that the facade of the Hurd House, unlike the Chapman House and the Humstone House, is not so much the property of an inflected body as it is the expression of a face incorporated into the landscape. Faces and heads are always bisymmetrical and allow only the limited taxonomy of contortions that we recognize as squinting, laughing, and grimacing. Perhaps the Hurd House is squinting at a place that is unusually bigger than life, although I must insist that the most dominant reading remains that of a typical and friendly small house seated inconspicuously on a mound in a sloping valley.

Fig. 14

The issue of seating a house on the land deserves some comment in regard to the architecture of Turner Brooks. In this respect the two-story, nearly quarter-circular "wall-roof" on the west side of the McLane House invites speculation about its purpose and its etymology as a shape unique to the architect (Fig. 14). If you were to discuss that curved apparition with its creator, you might be persuaded that it was descended from a metal cowling over a rumble seat or the front end of a steam locomotive chugging along the tracks. It appeared simultaneously on the prow and stern of Brooks's tiny Laffin House that he dragged on sled runners over the fields of Vermont. In this respect it emblematizes the energy and motion of a machine. Yet the McLane House is actually quite tranquil and "humanist" in appearance. We might ask whether this house is most informed by mechanistic, animistic, or domestic memories. Those multiple references are telling in respect to the many potent and venerable forms of architecture that upon inspection are revealed to be hybrid creations in which gods, mortals, trees, machines, and ancient temples are melted down and cast anew into uncanny forms of habitation or worship. The McLane House, like all of Turner Brooks's architecture, belongs to that tradition of hybridization. It is at once organic, mechanical, and, as always, ultimately domestic. However, it is in the latter respect, that of a proud domicile claiming the land on which it sits, that I see the curve as a *downward* rather than a horizontal sign of motion. It is a stomp on the ground underneath like the driving of a spear into the sand. It is a superb example of Turner Brooks being able to fix a sensitive building seemingly forever in a very specific place. As mobilized as those buildings may be in the mind of the poet, they dare you to move them one foot in the directions of front-back, left-right, or two inches up or down.

The Student

Turner Brooks was one of my first students after I began instructing in the first year at the Yale School of Architecture. Almost immediately he began to probe the power of the environment over the shaping of his buildings. He claimed a drafting table in one of the most sculptural corners of the concrete studio backed against a craggy wall and commanding a view of the entire class. His instructors were bent on encouraging the making of models, often in preference to drawings, as the best means of comprehending the three-dimensional space of architecture. Usually the students made models out of chipboard, but as the term evolved Brooks turned to plaster. From the beginning he wanted to site his buildings in the space of a world well beyond the prescribed lot line, and thus, when the assignment required the design of a small building-group, he began by constructing a contour model of an entire landscape incorporating villages, streets, and precipices, with hints of the "beyond."

The forces of the model took command as the terrain bubbled up on a piece of plywood the size of his drafting table. He knew that plaster was the ideal media for the constant addition and subtraction of forms. He discarded his triangles and mayline as his tools became chisels, bags of plaster, and buckets of water. Over time the wet plaster dripped over the edges as it was being mixed, and accumulated on the floor beneath the table in a manner that at least gave the impression of raising the floor, the table, and the developing project upward. Up went the mountains, and Brooks as well, until his drafting station became a shrine and a grotto. The emerging structure became connected to the drafting room, the hallways, the stairwells, and even the streets of New Haven as plaster footprints diverged and converged from all directions. Somehow I cannot remember the buildings he designed, but within the plaster landscape, I can recall geometric specks in the eye of the maelstrom that in their whiteness reminded me of a fabled Greek village.

Figs. 15, 16

When Brooks was not chiseling away on the whiteness of his model, he might very well have been found down by the blackness of the New Haven harbor at night making drawings of the great sooty behemoth that repeatedly erupted into plumes of steam and fire (Figs. 15, 16). The cranky condemned coke plant with its tilting conveyor belts, miniature elevated railroads, sheds, and stacks was living out its last few months before an act of demolition was to make way for a new electrical power plant. Night after night Brooks, Dan Scully, and one or two other classmates would admire and sketch the monstrosity as it approached its demise. I was told by an ecstatically dazed Brooks the morning after the final night that the faculty had erred by missing a once-in-a-lifetime chance to witness the workers and foremen of the coke plant speed up the trains, belts, and all the processes of the quarter-mile contraption to the breaking point until the last piles of coal had been consumed in a last wild frenzy of activity.

One might ask whether it is the soul of a sculptor, a draughtsman, a poet, or an architect that so enjoyed all that plaster, soot, geometry, and cacophony? One might also declare that such a question is faulty because it smacks of the professional categories and specializations that divide and weaken the art of architecture. We do know that Turner Brooks honors and practices all those disciplines in varying amounts and ways, as we know that he has chosen to spend the lion's share of his time designing and making buildings that incorporate the energies of each persuasion. In this respect he is more of a medievalist than a modernist. He remains the mythic Westerner who would stir music, mathematics, magic, and astronomy into a single pot.

His profound respect of the landscape is actually romantic and nineteenth-century as well. In the late twentieth century we have the fuel, machinery, and budget to manipulate and level the land as we hook buildings more directly to the burgeoning transportation infrastructure. Moreover, how many inhabitants want their consciousness raised about the nature of hills, valleys, or their orientation to the "Midwest" or the "Atlantic"? We are a modern, advanced, and technically endowed people with the capacity to look that stuff up on maps or sit back and watch it all whiz by on the virtual terrain provided by television.

But somehow all of that fails to explain why I feel both calm and troubled when I drive back down from Vermont or the hills of western Connecticut after visiting one of Brooks's works of architecture. His buildings calmed me down; but when I look to the left and right of the highway, I become disturbed by a perception that so much of our recent building seems to litter rather than to ennoble the world. As an incurable looker-at-buildings, I belong to that species that actually spends time outside, whether it be in the city, town, or the country. I believe that actual buildings and actual mountains still speak to us because they represent who we are, where we are, and because their conditions alert us to the fragility of civilization and the environment. It is in this respect that I find the buildings of Turner Brooks to be profound. His sensitive figures in the landscape have humility. They buttress my faith in the act and grandeur of architecture.

What is Once Well Done   Jonathan Schell

As children, Turner Brooks and I both attended what in those days was called a "progressive school," and in art class the teacher often would hand us large lumps of wet clay and tell us to make whatever we pleased with them. The day came when Brooks began to make his "ghost castles," by sticking his fingers in the clay from various angles until they touched in the middle, forming passages and rooms. Now Brooks is an architect, and I live with my family in one of his castles—a loft in New York City. It is perhaps not very surprising, then, that, seen at first glance, the loft he designed for us appears to be a kind of children's palace, and that the architect has stuck his fingers through the walls of the children's rooms to make secret passages between them. Yet even as the loft seems both to recall childhood and to be given over to children, as if it were a play-ground, it at the same time possesses in the highest degree such entirely unchildish qualities as exquisiteness of detail, formal beauty of line and proportion, and even a kind of splendor.

We live in an indoor, one-family city. In the back are three blue, peak-roofed children's rooms, each with a little window in front that looks out from a second-story sleeping loft. They are lined up along a back "street," or "alley," where the children "can wage gang warfare, and slash tires," as Brooks points out. Or they can climb a wall on the front side of the street to survey the adult proceedings on a central platform, which we think of as a stage, or, more pompously, as a public square. Or else they can race through any of four networks of passageways, each quite different from the others. These are: the small doors between the children's lofts; the tunnel-like, low, dark, book-lined passage to the kitchen area at the front of the loft; a simple, utilitarian hall, leading past the washer and dryer to the elevator; and the ramp, grandly widening as it spills down from the back "street" to the large, front area, with its row of six ten-foot-high windows. For anyone who wants quiet, there are two virtually self-contained suites in the back, each including a bathroom and a bedroom. One is a guest suite; the other is the master bedroom.

The double inside of the children's houses-within-a-house lends their rooms a double coziness. To lie on one of the children's beds high in one of the lofts, under a peaked roof, looking out the small window to the inside-outside, and, beyond that, through the six front windows to the true outside, is the very essence of coziness. Yet to look back from the front of the loft along the same line, letting the eye follow the colonnade to the stage, and then over the back wall to the skyline of little blue houses, is to experience the opposite of coziness: open space, public display, a touch of grandeur. Later, as I got to know Brooks's architecture better, I noticed that these two elements of our loft—on the one hand, a dim, labyrinthine, even burrow-like "private" realm, and, on the other, an open, light, gorgeously proportioned "public" space—occurred often in his work. Perhaps this catacombs/forum duality of Brooks's work stems from his early love of Grand Central Station, composed as it is of a lofty, classical central space from which tunnels extend in all directions. Both elements are present, for instance, in the McLane House and the Brooks House. In both, a many-leveled warren of chambers and passages, some tiny, others spacious, is clustered behind, or wrapped around, a spacious, airy living dining and kitchen area. In both, too, it is possible to peek back from the recesses of the burrow into the light— a possibility that sharpens the pleasurable contrast between the two. The exteriors of Brooks's houses often remind people of ships. The interiors also have ship-like qualities. The bedrooms— crowded against each other, with every inch accounted for and put to use—have something of the abbreviated- or compressed-house feeling of a ship's cabin, while the living space has the open atmosphere of a ship's deck—an atmosphere accentuated by the fact that the outer wall of both houses balloons out to one side, like a sail filled with wind.

The possibility of looking out from the privacy of the bedrooms into the public living space points to another similarity between our city-loft and many of Brooks's Vermont houses. Rather than radiating outward from a central point—say, a hall or vestibule—the spaces are arranged in a loop. They invite exploration. There is a certain involution in the design whereby the bedrooms turn back to afford the views of the living space. Perhaps this is one of the many reasons that the houses seem to act, like certain sculptures, not just optically, as an image on the eye, but physically, as a body on the body. Because motion in a loop is continuous, the explorations are potentially infinite. Investigating the back passages, one half hopes that, as in C.S. Lewis's *The Lion, the Witch, and the Wardrobe*, a closet wall will open onto a secret kingdom.

Both the exterior-like walls enclosed within the houses and the looping passageways contribute to the feeling of self-containment that strongly characterizes Brooks's houses. In our loft, the presence of the "street" and the children's houses make it seem as if the public realm has been pulled inside. In a manner of speaking, the outside world has been co-opted. In a time when life on the streets is harsh and dangerous, this appropriation makes sense. It gives the loft a feeling of independence from the world outside. Brooks's houses in the country also have an appearance of independence from their immediate surroundings. He has noted that the man-made, farmed, and fenced landscape that once fixed the place of the rural farm house and linked it to the world around it is quickly vanishing. His houses take their bearings, on the whole, from features of the natural landscape—rivers, hills, mountains—as ships do from stars. If, in spite of their likeness to moving things, Brooks's houses seem firmly placed in the landscape, the reason may be that their location is determined in relation to such primordially fixed landmarks as these.

Brooks, who makes use of some traditional Vermont building materials (clapboard siding, asphalt shingles, metal roofs), and who has lived in Vermont for a quarter of a century, has been called a vernacular architect, and there is truth in the description. Brooks's houses are highly appropriate to the Vermont landscape. On the other hand, there is nothing "nostalgic" about them. Any notion that they represent a longing for a vanished, more stable past is immediately rebutted by the houses' plain likeness to vehicles of all sorts, including cars and trailers. Here is no groping for American roots. And yet just for this reason the houses strike me as exceedingly American. There is more motion than stability in the history of the American landscape, which is continually being obliterated and rebuilt by what the economist Joseph Schumpeter called the "creative destruction" of the free market. The eclipse of agricultural Vermont that Brooks has noted and responded to in his bones is only one chapter in this story. How long, after all, was the American landscape fixed in the agricultural patterns of life that are now giving way to the shopping mall and forest alike? By European, not to speak of Asian, standards, the interval between the first settlement of the American wilderness and the cyclone of modern development has been brief.

Many believe that this cyclone has been an aesthetic calamity. If so, Brooks's houses stand out as exceptions. Yet they do not seek to repeal the modern world. They venture bravely, beautifully, and hopefully through it. Born, in part, of affectionate memories of movement, they are well-equipped to negotiate the swift currents of a world whose first law is unremitting change. Like any work of art—whether painting, music, or poem—that deals honestly and passionately with the confusions of the present day, Brooks's houses brighten the general scene. They give us assurance that we can be comfortable and at home not in some imaginary past but in *our* place and *our* time.

It makes sense that Brooks loves architectural models, which are of course entirely self-sufficient objects, having neither locations nor owners. He creates them in abundance for clients, at times whipping a variation of an existing plan together with the speed of a street-artist making a sketch. He presented our family with at least a half a dozen models in the course of designing our loft. Whole interiors were lifted out and replaced with subtly different ones even as we pressed our eyes to some miniature window. We all spent many hours peering through these windows, imagining ourselves walking down various tiny halls, cooking in tiny kitchens, sleeping in tiny beds. When children play in dollhouses or toy cities, they picture themselves living there. These models were toys that we *actually* would one day live in. And just as, peering into the models, we imagined our lives there, so, when we did live in the completed loft, there lingered the memory of a model.

Some of Brooks's models have in fact lifted free from any incarnation as dwellings. These models, which he calls "objects," exist for their own sake. The Lobsterman Houses are an example. They seem to have one foot in architecture and one in art, as monuments, for example, do. Someone *could* build one of these houses, but it's hard to imagine that anyone will.

One step farther along Brooks's Great Chain of Being (critics have noted the Medieval element in Brooks's work) are the Hovering Creatures. If the Lobsterman Houses have given utility the cold shoulder, the Hovering Creatures turn their back on it altogether. And yet, in their form and materials (clapboard, plywood), they remain resolutely architectural. Are they toys? They are not, though there is something of toys in them. Are they pieces of sculpture? The label seems wrong, although it would be hard to say why. Perhaps they are a modern version of the Roman Lares and Penates—households gods: the spirits of houses.

The objects cast light back on the houses. Brooks's houses, all observers agree, are polymorphic. It's hard to think of a single house of Brooks's that doesn't bear some resemblance to an animal, a vehicle, a machine, *and* a human being. Being polymorphic, they are also metaphoric. But the metaphors, unlike most of those in poetry, are reversible. (It works in poem to say that the moon was a ghostly galleon; it does not work to say that the ghostly galleon was a moon.) The houses do not only say that a house can be lobster-like; they also say that a lobster can be house-like, as can a boat, a coke plant, or a face. Thus, the Creatures and houses alike hover in more ways than one. They seem to hover a little above the spot they rest on; they hover between many animate and inanimate forms; and they hover over the world itself in the way that Plato, for one, thought that immaterial ideals hovered over physical reality, challenging it to attain perfection. The excitement one feels in the presence of Brooks's houses, it seems to me, flows in part from one's instant recognition in mind and body of these amazingly diverse references, which Brooks has somehow packed together into a disciplined, balanced, elegant—sometimes even austere—unity. And yet each house is unique. Each has the breath of life in it, and each possesses the unrepeatable individuality that characterizes living things. "Ideals of what? Perfect what?" one might ask. We cannot say, for we are in the world of art, not of philosophy or morals. Yet the word perfect is one that springs to mind when looking at several of Brooks's houses—a list that could begin with the McLane House, in Starksboro. These houses bring to mind the remark of another artist from New England. Thoreau said "what is once well done is done forever."

RESIDENTIAL PROJECTS

Glazebrook House   Bristol, Vermont   1972

Designed for a mother and son for both living and working (my design fee was paid with pots!), the Glazebrook House is sited in a gently rolling meadow on top of an esker that curls out of the woods into a field. The first floor has living, dining, and kitchen areas in one continuous space which connects to a pottery studio—a shed leaning up against the gabled element of the house—which in turn connects, by a trestle, to the kiln house. In the studio the pots are loaded onto a cart, wheeled out on small-gauge railroad tracks (rescued from a nearby abandoned brick plant), and into the kiln to be fired. The tracks extend the center line of the house and are visible from the living area through an interior window directly over the kitchen sink. One can stand, centered along this line, with a view across the studio and out along the tracks into the landscape beyond. From this point one feels some intimation that the house is being driven, gliding on the tracks, along the top of the esker. Upstairs are two bedrooms connected by a balcony space over the studio.

Approx. 1300 square feet (not including kiln house).

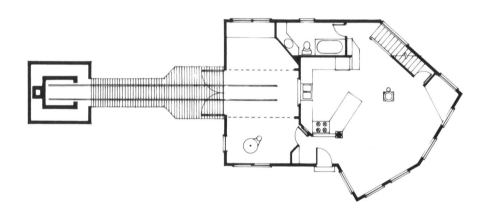

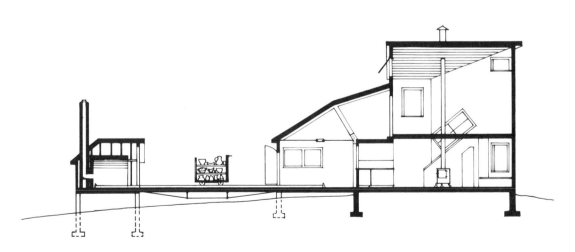

View of living room, first-floor plan and east-west section

South and north views

Borg House Middlebury, Vermont 1975

Designed for a small family, this house is built on a constricted site on a steep bank at the edge of a woods overlooking open fields to the north. The volume of the main space containing the living areas bends, contracts, and lifts up to receive the available south light coming in over the trees. One member of the family is a professional singer and the main space was designed to accommodate small informal recitals. Another is a professional photographer; the basement was designed as a darkroom.

1630 square feet.

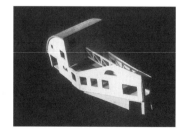

Brooks House   Starksboro, Vermont   1965–1982

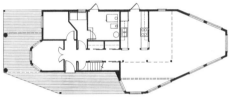

This house has undergone countless alterations, dismemberments, and additions. Starting as two tall and somewhat ruthlessly spare shed-roofed structures built eight feet apart, it evolved into a much more comfortable, squishier, more livable house over the years. Although completely transformed in exterior appearance, its history is imbedded inside—discovered in peculiar discontinuities of space and materials through which can be found strange passageways. Former parts of the original house can also be found, some still inhabited, in various corners of the surrounding landscape.

1640 square feet.

McLane House   Starksboro, Vermont   1976

This house is built in a weedy meadow on the edge of an agricultural landscape going to seed. Dining and kitchen areas sort themselves out within a single space that expands and contracts, somewhat like a bay window that grew dramatically to accommodate these functions of the house. Under the curved roof there is a bedroom and a stair to the second floor where a master bedroom looks over the living room below. A tiny twisting stair leads up to a third-floor loft where one inhabits the "brain" or "bridge" of the building. From there, looking past the dual chimneys, it is as if one were steering the house into the landscape beyond.

1620 square feet.

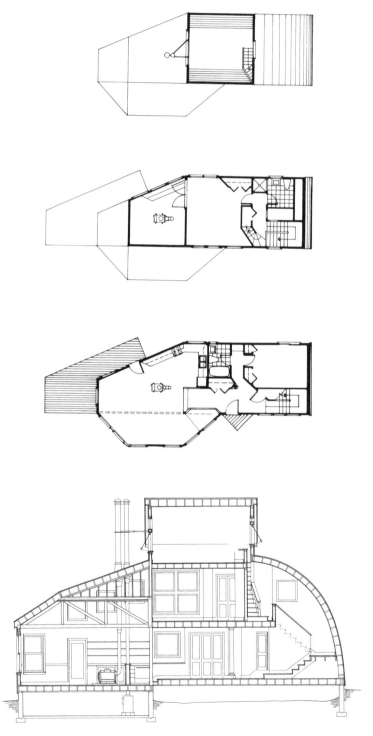

Plans and east-west section

Northwest and northeast views

Southeast and south views

West and southwest views

Hurd House Starksboro, Vermont 1981

This is a small house in a big landscape, built on a south-facing slope overlooking open fields and wooded hills that roll down into the Champlain Valley. I like to think it is a tiny house with "big" house moves. For example, the gentle slope of the gable spans the long dimension of the house while the porch roof stretches in one exaggerated gesture across the front facade. Like the neighboring little Greek revival houses, it uses scaled-up details, like the huge columns guarding the ends of porch, to enlarge its presence. The plan centers around a wood-burning stove: a bay window projects out in front, swelling out towards the view, a stair winds up behind, and the master bedroom, and even the bed, align along the same axis. The upstairs houses one large bedroom/ playroom and two tiny rooms that can be expanded at a later date with the addition of dormers.

1050 square feet.

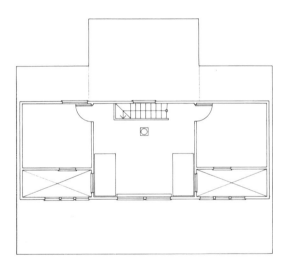

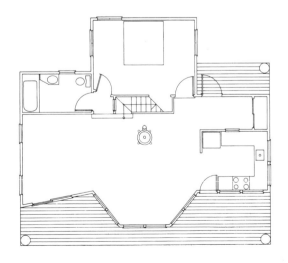

Opposite page: south view and plans
Above: north, south, and southeast views

Chapman House   Ferdinand, Idaho   1981

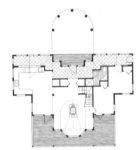

The Chapman House stands thrusting out between two huge Ponderosa pines on the last of a series of hills that break, wave-like, on the Camus Prairie in western Idaho. The rounded port-cochere accepts only smallish vehicles between its rough-hewn columns, while providing a deck for the master bedroom above. All rooms open into the brick-walled, two-story slot of space running the length of the south side of the building. This space allows light to penetrate deep into the main living areas. A porch wraps the north end of the house, giving views out over the prairie. The central north-south axis of the house, about which it is more or less symmetrical, lines up exactly (the builder sited it through his telescopic rifle site) with a railroad trestle two miles out into the prairie, the only visible man-made object out there in the waving prairie grasses.

1800 square feet.

Brown House New Canaan, Connecticut 1982

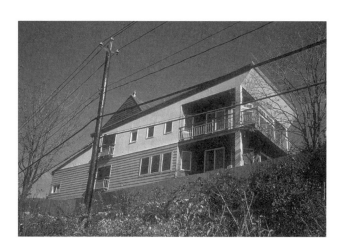

The intersection of a major road and a country lane form the narrow slot of land on which the Brown House fits—a little like a vehicle that did not clearly decide which route to take and comes grinding to a halt in the shrubbery, somewhere in between. This is a house for a couple who are both partially-retired doctors, sited overlooking the town to which both have administered their skills for many years. An office where patients can be seen was part of the program for the house.

3200 square feet.

Harris/Pesce House Sharon, Connecticut 1986

The Harris/Pesce House has two painting studio wings attached to a central "house" element. The studios spread out and funnel the landscape between them to make a south-facing court. The smooth painted boards of the house contrast with the more rustic, unpainted clapboards of the studios. The main living spaces look out through the bowed north wall to a landscape of rolling fields. A two-story slot of space on the south, behind the large window on the court side, allows light to penetrate deep into the dining and living room. Kitchen, study, and guest room occur at the junctions of the studio wings and house. The master bedroom is placed over the interior two-story space with the bed facing north, looking out the large double-hung window towards the view.

House: 1500 square feet; studios: 800 square feet each.

Peek House   Monkton, Vermont   1990

This house house is built on scruffy tundra-like grasses that slope down to a lake. The tower element housing bedrooms and bathrooms rises out of the corner of the single volume containing the living spaces. That volume sweeps out in an arc to view the lake and the landscape to the south, while presenting a tight, flat wall to the north. The ship-like models shown below rest tilted as if on mud flats, waiting for the tide to come in and float them off.

1610 square feet.

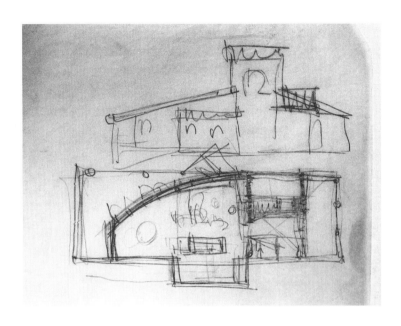

Study sketch and charcoal drawing

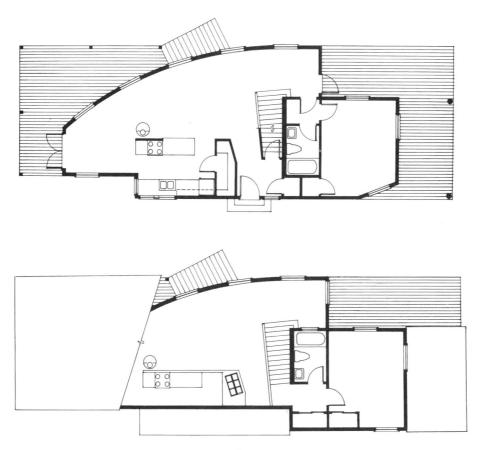

Plans

East and southeast views

West and southeast views

South view

Salvatore House   Sudbury, Vermont   1992–1994

Commissioned by a couple who have retired to the country with a great many books, this project was designed as both a house and a library with a two-story living room entirely wrapped with bookshelves. A third-floor tower study, reached by a narrow winding stair, is a retreat for reading and writing. The couple have seven grown children with families who visit often, inhabiting the guest rooms as well the adjacent little farmhouse and barn. The house was sited to link these two other buildings around a loosely defined exterior space that opens on the northwest to a magnificent view to the Champlain Valley.

2100 square feet.

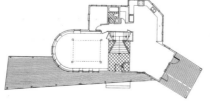

Lombard/Miller House   Westby, Wisconsin   1994

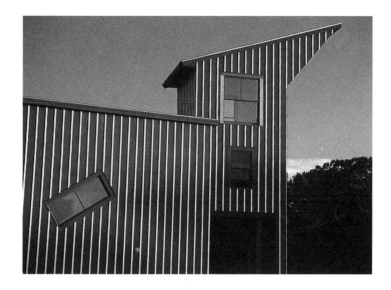

This house is sited in a gently rolling abandoned agricultural landscape. It stands at the edge of a woods of big old oaks overlooking a small meadowed valley through which a stream meanders sluggishly. Rounded hills slope up from all sides, some wooded, others with horizons of grass. Influenced by the Hovering Creatures (seen previously by the clients who claim them as a reason for choosing me as their architect), it has an insectile quality as if unfurling its wing as it walks across the landscape, pulling the studio behind. The first floor has living, dining, and kitchen areas all opening up to one another but differentiated by a level change of two steps. The steps define a make-shift stage between kitchen and living space to accommodate small-scale theatrical productions by family and friends. The second floor has a master bedroom, child's bedroom, bathroom, and balcony. A "lookout"/study is reached by a narrow stair that rises up behind the headboard of the master bed. This space looks out over the landscape under the up-tilted "brow" (see the Hovering Creatures) that seems to lead the house forward. The red and white board and batten stripes were derived from local Norwegian barns, while the creamy yellow of the clapboards is a color seen everywhere in this cream- and butter-producing landscape.

House: 2400 square feet; studio: 800 square feet.

West and south views

East and north views

Looking east from house to studio

Looking west from studio to house

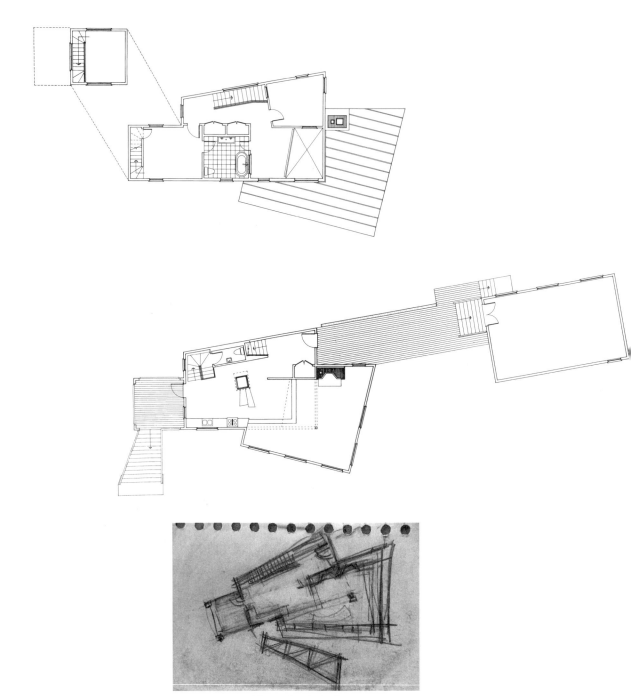

Plans and study sketch

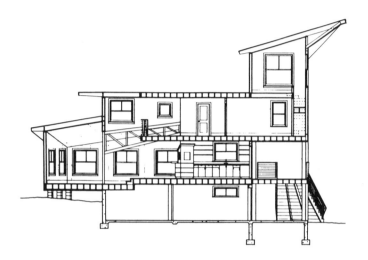

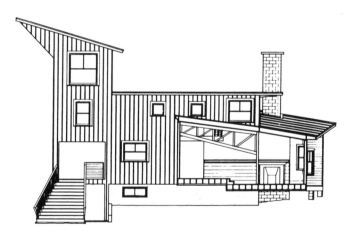

East–west section and south elevation

PUBLIC PROJECTS

Eugene O'Neill Theater   Provincetown, Massachusetts   1977

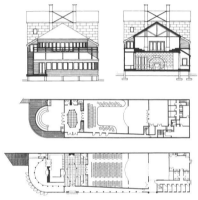

This project was designed during a five-day, charrette-style competition where the five invited teams of participants worked in the abandoned Flagship Restaurant, built on a pier a half-mile up the coast from the proposed project site. The program involved a simple theater with seating for four hundred, an archival library to house Eugene O'Neill original works, a community lounge/meeting room, and accommodations for a troupe of actors with a guest-star suite. The site was a forty-seven-foot-wide strip running some four-hundred feet in length between Commercial Street and the high water mark on the beach. Designed with Ross Anderson, the theater launches itself into the harbor with a pier and is anchored to the site by a large stone fireplace facing seaward that also serves to guard the entrance to the archives behind it.

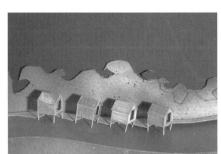
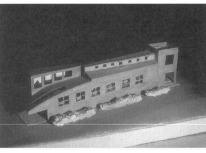
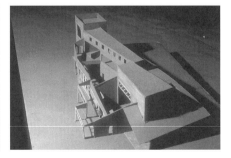

Skowhegan Studio and Arts Buildings   Skowhegan, Maine   1982

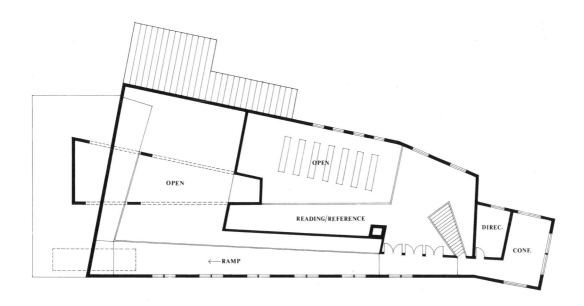

This project was an invited, five-day, on-site charrette modeled on the Eugene O'Neill Theater charrette a few years earlier. Again, five architects were selected and each could bring one associate, and again, I worked with Ross Anderson. The program included a central gallery/library/administrative facility as well as separate small sculpture and painting studios. Our building placed its stubby tower legs over the convergence of the old paths running through the campus. From there the building spread out its faceted body, forming a series of generous, well-lighted gallery and work spaces. On the north, the long, tall, straight wall ran parallel to the road; to the south the roofs sloped down to meet a meandering lower wall that defined an outdoor work and meeting space accessed through a multitude of garage doors. The rough, crude, asphalt flanks and metal roofs of this project would seem to have fit well with the existing functional buildings on the site. We designed the studios as simple shacks connected by a boardwalk at the edge of the woods.

Alley Stair   Burlington, Vermont   1983

This project consists solely of a public stair on a back alley to service offices on the second floor of a small commercial building. Both plan and section expand as the steps descend.

Interfaith Housing   Middlebury, Vermont   1990

This project, a subsidized affordable-housing complex built on a long, tapering, wedge-shaped piece of land running west of a railroad line, consists of thirty individual two- and three-bedroom units organized in six buildings grouped around two commons. The back doors and decks of each unit open onto these spaces, with views out to the Adirondack Mountains to the west. The front doors face out towards parking and the access road, which runs parallel to the railroad tracks. A path cuts through the center of each of the buildings, connecting the two open spaces to one another and to the parking. Each building ends in a public porch.

Gates Center, College of the Atlantic   Bar Harbor, Maine   1992

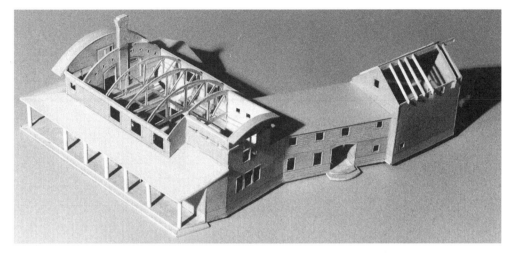

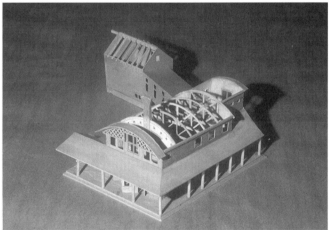

This building has squirmed its way, bending and flexing, into a site constricted by other buildings, an access road, and existing trees, to form the south wall of a court that exists at the very center of the campus. The Gates Center is designed to house the diverse, collective activities of the school. The main body of the building is a space that can accommodate all-school meetings as well as drama, music, dance, talks, poetry readings, and other public events. A wing of faculty offices connects to a small gallery with a lecture hall underneath.

9600 square feet.

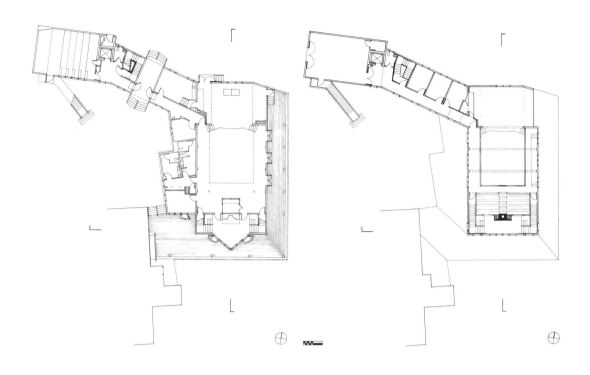

First- and second-floor plans, north-south section

*Clockwise, from top left: gallery, auditorium (from stage),
fireplace detail, auditorium (from balcony)*

Stair detail and north view

South and northeast views

OBJECTS

—Rome 1984—

Initially conceived as a 25-foot-high construction, this monument, a sort of cross between an obelisk and a pyramid translated into wood, suddenly shrank to human size and simultaneously sprouted wings. These last not only gave it mobility but also lent an angelic, Christian element to its pagan origins. To commemorate this small miracle, its original Etruscan name—*Grotto Ferrocco Tusculanus*—was changed, and it was baptized and christened "Il Risorgimento."

As construction progressed, I began to realize that this shape was derived from many important objects I have known all my life. It was the shape of a stone tower marking the entrance to a harbor in Maine; it was the clapboard top to the firehouse in a small town in Vermont. It was also the tiny electric engine that pushed the great "hot car" at the coke plant in New Haven, and it was the bell buoy off the New England coast that I have sailed by numerous times in the fog.

Top to bottom, left to right: A Buoy, Changing the Course of History, Contemplation of Suicide, Important Visit, The Annunciation, Crisis in the Suburbs, In Heaven with St. Ivo, Spawning Progeny

The drawings show various derivations and reincarnations of Il Risorgimento. Among the first are those which relate to its origin as a buoy and engine, and the "Important Visit" to see the pyramids. Among the last are its "Contemplation of Suicide," images of responding to calls of distress, and finally those where, in a fit of inflamed egotism, I saw it not only as the agent of the Annunciation, but also in heaven with Borromini's St. Ivo, where it gleefully spawns progeny of its own. Later during my summer in Rome, the monument made a series of appearances around the city. There was a dawn visit to the Piazza Navona where, with nothing but pigeons as spectators, it confronted a real obelisk. At midday it mounted the steps of the Campidoglio to wistfully contemplate the vacant base of the statue of Marcus Aurelius. It went on to look in on Bramante's Tempietto, continued up the Gianicolo to pay its respects to Garibaldi, glided through the Piazza del Popolo at dusk, and was awash in the Trevi Fountain by nightfall.

If Il Risorgimento does not soon disappear in an apocalyptic puff of smoke, a final resting spot will be sought. I imagine this will be a rocky outcropping of one of the Alban Hills which looks out over a large slice of landscape with Rome in the distance. Here the elements will go to work, peeling off the paint, warping the slats, stripping off the wings. There will be a time, perhaps, before vanishing off the face of the earth altogether, when bleached and weathered, and the wood become like dried old bones, that its pagan origins may claim it again, and it will be more like a monument than ever before.

Clockwise, from top left: a history lesson, on the steps of San Quirinale,
in the Piazza del Popolo, leaving the American Academy

Top to bottom, left to right: climbing the steps of the Campidoglio, the used car salesman, in the Acqua Paulo, at San Pietro, in the Piazza Navona, in Campo dei Fiori, receiving advice from the Garibaldini, cavorting in the gardens of the the Villa Aurelia

Hovering Creatures Burlington, Vermont 1989

—Burlington 1988—

The winged creatures are descendants of Il Risorgimento; they have evolved to become more directional and horizontally elongated, partly in response, no doubt, to the vaster spaces of this side of the world. Inherently furtive and restless like their ancestor, they like flitting and hovering over newly cut hay fields like fireflies—dusk and twilight being their favorite hours. They are seen in pairings, small flocks, and occasionally in solitude. Migrating between city, suburb, and country, they enjoy both urbanity and rusticity. On cold winter nights they have been known to enter a house and draw up close to the hearth in front of a crackling fire. There they will stretch and flounce their wings, jostle each other in a kind of merry camaraderie, and one wonders, if with the warming of their blood, they are experiencing some wistful vision of the sunny, warm Mediterranean climate, and the old civilization in which their ancestor cavorted about not so long ago.

Lobsterman Houses   Burlington, Vermont   1989

Although they were originally conceived for a particular client and site (a brother, on a wet marsh by the ocean), these models have taken on a peculiar life of their own and have evolved with no particular full scale project in mind, the client having evolved into an imaginary retired lobster-man. Tiny cardboard grasshopper-like objects have spawned larger amphibious offspring that inhabit various appropriately wet spongy landscapes on the property where I live.

Furniture

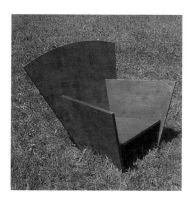  

Top to bottom, left to right:
Dining Chair 1 (Harris/Pesce House), Dining Chair 2 (Lombard/Miller House), Lawn Chair
Arm Chair (Lombard/Miller House), Lamp, Bed (Lombard/Miller House)
Speeding Chaise Lounge, Dining Table (Lombard/Miller House)

AFTERWORD

Moving Images (Tales from Asphaltum) Ross Anderson New York City 1994

Turner Brooks has always sought out the dark, the smoldering and the atmospheric. Soot, tar, burning tires, old factories, asphalt shingles, and whirring steam engines are among his muses. He would prefer that all of his structures were belching smoke and flames like a phalanx of horrible machines, engaged in their own, primitive, volcanism.

His buildings suggest movement and direction and house a strange, quivering, bent space inside, shaped by torque, tension, and pressure. These structures are vectors, with exteriors that are tough and taut, with big bones, backs, noses, and large, bellows-like lungs. They are not gentle. Their stretched skins of asphalt shingles or narrow boards, wrap buildings that are always *doing* something. Grinding, dragging, slipping, squeezing, or pushing, they don't sit still. His one constructed monument has been driven through the streets of Rome on the back of a small delivery truck. It appeared unannounced, in empty piazzas at dawn and in churning fountains at dusk, challenged by the *carabinièri*, flapping its arms like some great bird seeking a stabile perch. Christened *Il Risorgimento*, it now resides in the hills of Umbria, among Etruscan shards.

Rusted models of cars, tin boats, old toy trucks, and chrome hood ornaments, with shared qualities of speed and direction, gather in his studio. Past generations of sketch models are revered, as ancestral bones and relics might be in some great, dusky hall. Rather than rationally composed, they come from somewhere deep in the gut and the heart. He coaxes them out of scraps of cardboard and globs of glue, bending and peering and pulling, as if these actions could instill some life into the nascent structures. A kind of reverse voodoo that imparts rather than takes life away. Rubbing, bending, painting, and sanding, agonizing over the proper hue or shade. It is as if he were trying to make fire from flint and tinder, or from two dry sticks. "Bend down and look through this from right *here....*"

Skiing on trails through the woods or skating on frozen ponds at midnight as coyotes howl in the distance, *always* moving through the trees and in between hills, finding cozier spaces that lie where the land folds. Here, myths exist, and shepherds, shepherdesses, hamadryads, satyrs, and nymphs roam. His frequent teaching keeps him sliding through the landscape like a weird shark, needing the constant movement to force images through him. Listening to Dostoevsky on tape and driving a favored vehicle through the palpable darkness, as if inhabiting the twisted, layered moodiness of a Ryder painting.

Notice the slight lumbering motion of his houses. They *do* move, but perhaps only at night, when the fields and roads are empty. They manage to drag themselves about, searching for their creator, who is probably setting a length of dirt road on fire, pursuing his own personal fictions.

Acknowledgements

Since the idea of publishing a book on my work was first presented to me, I have had my essay and project descriptions nested self-consciously in my word processor under "Narcissism" and later, under "Casaubon," the lugubrious and egotistical character in George Eliot's *Middlemarch*. It can only be seen as feeding the narcissism that the authors of all of the essays in this book are actually my old friends. Although I have had many sweating doubts about whether all of this is a good idea, I will now have to leave it to others to take a more critical view of the work. I can, however, take this opportunity to credit some who have been important and influential to both my work and to the book.

Two contemporaries, Dan Scully and Ross Anderson, have been important as teachers and critics and inspiration. Their opinions about design issues, when I get stuck, are ultimately the ones I trust. Dan taught me much about tautness, speed, and bending space. (I acknowledge that his buildings, always in the fast lane, are speedier than mine.) Ross has been my collaborator on several competitions and on some of the other projects included in this book.

Other very important figures in my development as an architect are Vincent Scully, who first inspired me with the idea that a building could relate to the distant and larger landscape, i.e. the Horns of Hymettus; Robert Venturi, who assured me that a gable was okay and that the outside of a building could cloak mysteries inside; Charles Moore, who accepted enthusiastically some of my student work (under another regime it is likely I would have been quickly thrown out of school); Kent Bloomer, my great teacher at architecture school, who first informed me that there was such a thing as *space* and that it was a physical thing which could be formed, molded, and shaped. Mike Burgess and Peter Laffin are the master carpenters and wonderfully skilled builders who taught me that clapboards, corner boards, frieze boards, and a roof with a soffit and a fascia were not only sensible but also could look good. None of these projects would have been possible without the assistance of the stalwart members of my office, a list that includes, over a span of some twenty years, Mike Cadwell, Michael Hassig, Stuart Hamilton, Greg Clawson, Peter Herman, Dennis Willmott, and Tom Warner. Over the last few years Tom Carey has been the steady ballast in a practice which goes up and down.

In regard to this book I want to thank Kent Bloomer, Jonathan Schell, and Ross Anderson for so generously contributing their essays. In regard to my own essay, Martha Finney greatly helped and encouraged me. Discussions with Beth Humstone and her thoughts and critical observations have made my writing much more truthful.

I wish to thank Kevin Lippert of Princeton Architectural Press and Julie Iovine, who had the idea to do this book in the first place. I am very grateful to be the recipient of a generous grant from the Graham Foundation, which was crucial to the book's implementation. Finally, the skill and patience of Allison Saltzman, who did the final editing and design at PAP, is incredibly appreciated.

I would like to dedicate the work in this book to my mother, who gave me endless encouragement with the making of things in my youth.

—Turner Brooks

Project Chronology

LOMBARD/MILLER HOUSE	1994
SALVATORE HOUSE	1992–94
GATES CENTER	1992
ROCKWELL HOUSE	1992
INTERFAITH HOUSING	1990
PEEK HOUSE	1990
HOVERING CREATURES	1989
LOBSTERMAN HOUSES	1989
HARRIS/PESCE HOUSE	1986
SCHELL LOFT	1986
FUISZ HOUSE	1985
IL RISORGIMENTO	1984
ALLEY STAIR	1983
BROWN HOUSE	1982
HUMSTONE HOUSE	1982
SKOWHEGAN BUILDINGS	1982
CHAPMAN HOUSE	1981
HURD HOUSE	1981
CHELMINSKI HOUSE	1978
EUGENE O'NEILL THEATER	1977
LAFFIN HOUSE	1976
McLANE HOUSE	1976
BORG HOUSE	1975
GLAZEBROOK HOUSE	1972
BROOKS HOUSE	1965–82

Photography Credits

ERIK BORG
p. 16 (fig. 12), p. 20 (fig. 22), p. 55 (top), p. 56, p. 127 (top left and right)

SCOTT FRANCES/ESTO
p. 34 (figs. 3, 6, 7, 8), p. 74, p. 78, p. 79, p. 80, p. 81 (bottom)

PAUL FERRINO
p. 57 (top right), p. 66, p. 69 (top), p. 71 (bottom right)

WAYNE FUJII
p. 30 (fig. e), p. 57 (top left)

GALLERY JOE, PHILADELPHIA
p. 104 (top), p. 147

MICK HALES
p. 72, p. 73

DOOJIN HUANG
p. 29 (fig. 36a)

TIMOTHY HURSLEY
p. 38 (fig. 10a)

ROBERT PERRON
p. 21 (fig. 25), p. 52, p. 53, p. 54, p. 55 (bottom)

CERVIN ROBINSON
front cover, p. 18 (fig. 15), p. 58, p. 59, p. 61, p. 62, p. 84, p. 86, p. 87, pp. 90–94

DENNIS SPARLING
p. 19 (fig. 20)

BRIAN VANDEN BRINK
p. 25 (fig. 31b), p. 106, pp. 109–111

MICHAEL WISNIESKI
p. 14 (fig. 6)

All other images courtesy of Turner Brooks

Bibliography

1994

"Caught in the Act: Architect Turner Brooks of Vermont, USA." *Monthly Review of Architecture* (August 1994), pp. 72–80.

"News/Projects." Lombard/Miller House. *Progressive Architecture* (June 1994), p. 69.

"Wisconsin House." Lombard/Miller House. *Global Architecture* no. 41 (April 1994), pp. 32–33.

"Creature of Context." Gates Center, College ofthe Atlantic. *Architectural Record* (January 1994), pp. 66–71.

1993

"Wochenend-Und Ferienhaus Nur Auf Den Ersten Blick." Peek House. *Hauser* (February 1993), pp. 28–35.

1992

Peek House. *Architectural Record* Record Houses issue (April 1992), pp. 96–101.

1991

"World's 100 Foremost Architects." *Architectural Digest* AD 100 issue (August 1991), pp. 52–53.

"Let's Play House." Schell Loft. *Metropolitan Home* (March 1991), p. 73.

1990

"Three Houses and Drawings." Harris/Pesce, Fuisz, and Sheldon Houses, charcoal drawings. *Global Architecture* no. 29 (July 1990), pp. 148–159.

1989

"Making Home Work." Harris/Pesce and Glazebrook Houses. *Metropolis* (March 1989), pp. 60–65.

"Casa Per Due." Harris/Pesce House. *Casa Vogue* (May 1989), pp. 204–207.

"An American Mythmaster." Harris/Pesce and Fuisz Houses. *Metropolitan Home* (December 1989), pp. 92–98.

1988

"Americana con brio." Fuisz House. *Architectural Record* Record Houses issue (April 1988), pp. 96–105.

"A House for Two Artists." Harris/Pesce House. *Architectural Record* Record Houses issue (April 1988), pp. 96–105.

1987

"The Analogous and the Anomalous Architecture of the Everyday." McLane, Hurd, and Fuisz Houses. *Ottagono* (September 1987), p. 28.

"An Exhibition." Sheldon House. *Places: A Quarterly Journal ofEnvironmental Design* vol. 4, no. 4 (1987), pp. 38–39.

1986

"A Sense of Place." Hayes House addition. *The New York Times* Home Design Magazine (April 1986), front cover, p. 4, p. 20.

Architectural League of New York, *Emerging Voices: A New Generation ofArchitects in America* (New York: Princeton Architectural Press, 1986); McLane House, pp. 98–99.

1985

"Roman Holiday." Il Risorgimento. *Architectural Record* (January 1985), pp. 74–75.

"A Portfolio of Projects." *Architectural Record* (August 1985), pp. 118–129.

Duo Dickenson, *The Small House* (New York: McGraw-Hill, 1985); McLane House, pp. 44–51.

Donald Prowler, *Modest Mansions* (Emmaus, PA: Rodale Press, 1985), Glazebrook, Hurd, and McLane Houses.

1984
Duo Dickenson, *Adding On* (New York: McGraw-Hill, 1984); Hayes House addition.

1982
"Architecture: Turner Brooks." Chelminski House. *Architectural Digest* (February 1982), pp. 112–119.

1981
"Recent New England School Buildings." Green Mountain Valley School. *Architectural Record* (June 1981), pp. 112–117.
"Chelminski House." *Global Architecture* no. 8 (Spring 1981), pp. 150–154.
Gerald Allen and Richard Oliver, *Architectural Drawing: The Art and the Process* (New York: Whitney Library of Design, 1981); charcoal drawings, pp. 166–169.

1980
"Charles Moore and Company." Borg, Glazebrook, McLane, and Solworth Houses. *Global Architecture* no. 7 (fall 1980), pp. 96–205.
"Eight for the Eighties." McLane House. *Texas Architecture* (July/August 1980), p. 69.

1979
"Haus Butterworth." Butterworth House. *Baumeister* (December 1979), p. 1103.
"House Butterworth." Butterworth House. *Stern* (September 1979), p. 155.
"Zwei Houser in Vermont." Glazebrook and Higgins Houses. *Baumeister* (July 1979), pp. 698–700.

"A Cast of Characterizations for a Playhouse on Cape Cod." Eugene O'Neill Theater. *Architectural Record* (March 1979), pp. 129–138.
"Architecture: Turner Brooks." McLane House. *Architectural Digest* (January/February 1979), pp. 116–123.
"Maison Glazebrook." Glazebrook House. *L'Architecture d'Aujourd Hui* (January 1979), p. 93.

1977
"The Shape of Things to Come." Laffin House. *House and Garden* (Winter 1977).

1976
"Signals." Glazebrook House. *House and Garden* (Fall 1976), pp. 72–73.

1975
"What More Could a Good House Be?" Butterworth and Glazebrook Houses. *Architectural Record* (January 1975), pp. 105–110.

1974
Vincent Scully, Jr., *The Shingle Style Today, or The Historian's Revenge* (New York: George Braziller, 1974); Butterworth, Glazebrook, and Higgins Houses.

1973
"Twin Towers." Brooks House. *House and Garden* (Winter 1973), p. 56.

I have always loved the fragile little wood-frame house standing out there, confronting the large landscape alone. Light glows from the window, and one senses the interior space as a delicate vessel floating in the night, the hills menacing and black, looming, and kept at bay.

There are times in the fog when suddenly the dark hulk of the house rises out of the ground, its interior glowing and warm, chimneys sending smoke out hissing into the atmosphere.

There are times when the blizzard howls outside, lights shine like headlights out into its blurring fury, and we sit cozily watching…and heaping more wood on the fire.

There are times when the Hovering Creatures are floating and cavorting about the moonlit landscape in the tall grass amongst the flickering of fireflies and breaths of humid air. Across a stone wall is the shape of a looming, dark vessel gliding silently across a luminescent meadow.

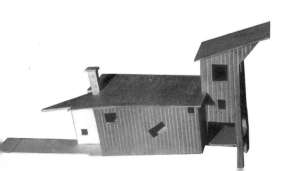